I0481001

The Left Behind Millennial

Business Formation Simplified

Siji Olufunwa

Dedication

I dedicate this book to my sweet boy Simeon. I pray I do
you justice as your mom.
To my amazing husband, Seun, who is always
ready to take a leap of faith with me. To my dad for teaching
me to think wisely.
To my mom for encouraging me to keep, keeping on.
To all my day ones and biggest supporters.
And to the generations denied
the chance to have a chance to change the world.

TO:

FROM YOUR CHEERLEADER:

A GIFT TO HELP MAKE YOUR DREAMS COME TRUE!

Introduction

When my husband and I opened our first business in 2017 and a second one in 2018, we were unsure what we were doing.

Starting a business seems like a mystery at first, especially when you do not know which steps to take. Many people are afraid to take that crucial first step because of fear of the unknown, fear of failure, or even fear of success. These fears hold most of us back.

Everyone faces roadblocks when starting a business. Our main challenge was the lack of a simplified guide that could empower us with the appropriate knowledge to grow our start-ups. The high start-up failure rate and an inability to make it beyond the first few steps have been primarily linked to a lack of actionable and relevant information in business.

Information is power. Information is an asset for anyone who has yet to master the skills necessary for profitability and success. Running a profitable business is more than simple metrics. It is more than just knowing your bank account balance, revenues received, and amounts payable.

We have learned so much throughout our entrepreneurship journey, which is the main reason I'm writing this book. I want to share the information that I have accumulated over time, and during the establishment of our businesses. My goal is to simplify the process for any person who may be stuck in a rut, not knowing where to start, as well as those who have just started and do not know which step to take next.

Generally, an estimated 600,000 businesses are started across the U.S. every year. Sadly, for every American that starts an actual business, millions of others only start another new year with the resolution: *Okay, this is my year, I am finally going to start my business…* except, they don't.

Sadly, many people, both young and old, are stuck in dead-end jobs without the courage to do something they are passionate about because they do not know where and how to start. Why would you want to labor under the weight of mediocrity all your life? Don't you desire to break free and shine like the star you are by doing what you love?

Running a successful business does not require that you reinvent the wheel. Many people spend so much time thinking about how to start the most unique business. Many people find it overwhelming to start a business because they believe they need to start from scratch.

You already have what it takes: you can turn your talents and hobbies into a unique, high-value, profitable business. The goal is to understand the business formation process, then identify a market share that creates an opportunity for the things you love and fill that gap.

In the next chapters, I will break down the business formation steps and present them in an understandable and simplified guide for the benefit of everyone who does not know how or where to start. You will learn all the details and processes that you need to follow and how you can take action, starting from this moment.

You are about to create an asset. You are about to be liberated and empowered.

Let's begin!

ISBN: 979-8-728-45582-0

Table of Contents

About me

My name is Siji Olufunwa, and I am a passionate entrepreneur. My husband, Seun, and I have started two different businesses. In 2017, we commenced my husband's service-based firm, Event Staffing Team, which primarily provides professional event staffing throughout the DFW Metroplex in Texas. In 2018, we founded and registered my skincare brand ShySeven, LLC, which is product/E-commerce based.

With both enterprises, we were learning as we go. We were the ones researching how and where to register our businesses, where to find the resources we would need for operations, inventory, graphic designers, an attorney, and so on. We looked into everything ourselves.

Why am I writing this book?

We had no simplified guides available to advise us to do this or that. Throughout the formation of our businesses, we learned so much that we can now pass on to others. I want to make the process of business formation easier for others by creating an understandable and simplified blueprint of simple steps.

I will provide you with reliable information on the topic of business formation. I have read extensively, researched widely, and consulted many professionals so that you do not have to. I will show you how to hack the business formation process to create a profitable business.

Who is this book meant for?

Forbes reported that approximately 20-40% of Americans dislike their jobs. Many people are stuck in jobs they despise. It's sad, waking up every morning with the feeling that your career has stalled and there is no prospect of career growth. This is no way to live.

This book is meant for everyone who wants to take a chance on themselves and lift themselves out of their rut. Many people dream of starting a business but don't know how or where to start.

This book will help you prepare yourself for the next step, identify business prospects, and take advantage of opportunities that present themselves. Of course, you will have to overcome some basic challenges, but the rewards of going after your dreams will truly be worth it.

What will be covered in this book?

This book explores the process of business formation exhaustively. You may be passionate about starting your business, but you may be lacking a sense of direction.

I have pulled together all the necessary information to help you form your own business. These pages cover the 12 most important business formation steps no one will tell you about. I know from experience because we had to do it on our own. Most books provide generalized information, but no one will break it down for you, as does *The Left Behind Millennial: Business Formation Simplified*.

Use everything provided in this book as a jumping-off point to fire yourself up and start your journey right away.

STEP 1.

Step 1. Is your Business a Service or a Product?

Marketing techniques, running costs, and initial capital are just a few ways that a service business varies from a product business. At the core, the main difference is that product-based businesses deal with physical, tangible goods while a service-based business sells skills, expertise, and intangible time.

Understanding a product-business and a service-business

A product business displays items in a physical location or online so that customers can view them. Customers have an opportunity to touch or see the products before they buy.

Examples include:

- Consumer goods: clothes, beauty products, home equipment, etc.
- Agricultural products: vegetables, dairy, cereals, etc.
- Technological products: cameras, phones, laptops, etc.

Serviced-based businesses may or may not operate from a physical location. Depending on the service offered, the physical location may be necessary or irrelevant. They are typically less expensive to operate, and the price of the services may also vary depending on many factors, including experience, location, and the amount of time it takes to deliver the service.

Examples include:

- Personal care: therapists, hairstylists, etc.
- Healthcare: doctors, nurses, etc.
- Creative services: event staffing, graphic designers, etc.

Why does it matter?

To satisfy your customers, you must understand the type of business that you run and the customers' needs in that niche.

Understand your competitors and what your potential customers are looking for. Only then will you be able to compete and satisfy your customers at their point of need.

When you finally understand the trends of your business and the feedback you receive, you will be able to make adjustments to your strategies and outdo your competitors.

❖ Use the note section below to jot down any relevant thoughts or ideas related to your service/product-based business.

Notes :

_____

_____

_____

_____

_____

_____

_____

STEP 2.

Step 2. Choose a great business/ brand name.

The first thing customers interact with is the name of your brand. Your brand name has to be authentic, distinctive, and memorable. Your target audience should be able to relate to it. It should be something that sticks in their mind and helps to build and maintain trust.

A strong brand name is vital to building and maintaining a strong reputation. And who doesn't want that?

What is your business/ brand name?

Your brand name does not have to be limited to what your business is about. You can use punchy imagery and taglines to come up with a clever name that represents your brand.

Here are some common brands that did not limit their brand name to the services they offer:

- Google
- Amazon
- Nike
- Adidas
- Target

A name builds a strong brand reputation.

Pick a name that mirrors the tone of voice for your brand. You should research widely and have a deep understanding of your target market. You must not take this lightly because so many variables depend on your brand's name.

❖ Jot down a few catchy business names and think them over for a bit. Then select one to move on to the next step.

```
Notes :
_____
_____
_____
_____
_____
_____
_____
```

Avoid complex names that are hard to spell, say or read. If your friends fumble to pronounce it, maybe you should use another name. Take your time selecting the right name. Think it over and make sure you feel confident with the name you have chosen.

• You might consider your logo design idea after selecting a name. A logo is a visual representation of your vision and is a big part of your identity as a brand. A good logo must be unique and memorable. It should also differentiate your brand from all your competitors and any other person in general.

STEP 3.

Step 3. Purchase a Domain.

What is a Domain?

Your website needs an address where internet users can gain access to it. This address is the domain name. A domain is the actual presence of your website on the internet. When people type this address into their search engine, they can visit your website. Every domain is unique. Two websites can never have the same domain.

For users to access it, a domain must first be registered. Once you have a domain name, you will need to host it first before you can launch your website. Once you do this, your website will be accessible on the internet.

How and where to get a Domain name for my business?

To get a domain name, use sites like Google Domains, GoDaddy, or Namecheap. Type in the name you would like for your domain. If it is available, pay for it. Not all domain names will be available. You will only be able to buy a domain name that another person has not registered yet.

Make sure it is catchy and unique, so people are more likely to remember it and type it into their browsers. You can also search for commonly searched words in your niche and incorporate them into your domain name.

Gold Tip: Some of these domain sites will allow you to create a business email and a website. There may be an additional fee, but it's highly recommended that you at least consider creating the business email for a more professional look. For example, your business email may look a little something like info@yourbusinessname.com.

This is a great way to build trust when emailing customers or offering a contact method instead of your personal email that ends with @gmail.com or @yahoo.com.

I will return to websites later, but I wanted to mention that these domain sites do offer those services for you as well.

❖ Check out different domain sites and write down the pros and cons of each. Then, select the domain site that best fits your business needs and purchase your domain.

Notes :

_____
_____
_____
_____
_____
_____
_____

STEP 4.

Step 4. Obtain your social media accounts and platforms.

A strong social media presence leads to successful business marketing. Your brand name must be consistent across all your social media platforms. Social media is the easiest and most affordable way to market your business and put it in front of a large audience, millions if not billions of people.

Why social media is crucial for the growth of your business.

- Social media builds a community.

You will build awareness for your brand, create engagement with that community and attract new customers. You will be able to speak with your clients and customers on a personal level, no matter where they may be in the world.

You can also advertise, sell your products, and spread the word about special events and promotions.

- **Social media gives your business an online presence.**

It may be indirect, but social media creates a platform where people can share content such as blogs, pictures, products and services, promotions, etc. When your content is shared, it ranks higher on search engines. Social media platforms are search engines themselves; for example, Facebook has over 2 billion users.

With platforms such as these, you can show up whenever customers need you.

- **Social media advertising is more targeted and less expensive**

On Facebook, you can use the information available — age, profession, gender, purchasing pattern, and behavior, to target a specific audience. Doing this requires very little time, and you can spend as little as $20 to do so.

Here are some links to social media platforms with large followings:

Instagram: 500 million active users daily.

Facebook: 1 billion active users daily.

Twitter: 353 million active users monthly.

YouTube: 2 billion users monthly.

LinkedIn: over 260 million active users.

Pinterest: perfect for brands targeting women.

Snapchat: is the best platform to target generation Z, with over 60% of its users under 24.

TikTok: 689 million users with 80 million in the US alone.

Gold Tip: You need your brand name to match everywhere across social media accounts where you want to broadcast your business. Not every social media platform will be for you but you should create accounts for the ones you know will benefit your business the most and hold your name on them.

Personal Note: I registered my skincare business in 2018, but I did not officially launch my business or create content on my social media accounts until 2020. But I made the accounts ahead of time to hold my name because I knew eventually, I would be creating content for my business there.

What social media platforms would work best for your business?

Notes :

_____

_____

_____

_____

_____

STEP 5.

Step 5. You Need a Business Plan

A business plan articulates the strategies necessary for the execution of your business ideas. A business plan provides a clear roadmap on the steps that should be taken, the amount and availability of resources, and the timeline for the results to be anticipated.

Why do you need this living document?

With a clear business plan, you will be able to track your progress in line with the goals you have laid out. Business plans can also attract investors. With a clear business plan, investors can evaluate your business and determine if it is worth investing in.

A business plan will help you:

- Make critical decisions in tough times.
- Create a realistic vision. It will also help you figure out and fill in any gaps in your strategy.
- Avoid major mistakes that may cost you your business.
- Prove that your business is viable.
- Set, communicate, and benchmark your objectives.
- Guide service providers.
- Secure finances from investors.
- Reduce general risks.

- Understand the broader business landscape.

How to create a business plan?

You can try a downloadable business plan template or try free places to easily create a business plan, such as Google Docs. If you have a Google account, Google docs is free and readily available for you to use for creating, saving, and storing your documents. Create a Google Account

Tips for creating your business plan: To complete a detailed plan, keep these questions in mind:

Who? What? When? Where? Why? How?

- Who are the owners, managers, partners for the business?
- What does the business do? What is your service or products?
- When are you starting the business? When is the service or product available? When do you anticipate scaling?
- Where is the business located? Is it in multiple locations? Is it online? Is it in a set location?
- Why are you doing the business?
- What is the purpose behind this specific business? For example, I am writing a book with step-by-step instructions on how to start a legal business. The purpose is to create a simple business formation guideline for other entrepreneurs to follow and create their own business.

Additional considerations for planning your business:

- How do you plan to fund the business?

- How do you plan to run the business? Online? In brick-and-mortar location?
- How do you plan to structure the business?

Gold Tip: Enter the information you already know into your business plan. For example, you may know who the business owners will be, but you may not know the overall cost or estimate it will cost to run your business right away. Remember, the business plan is a living document, so you can go back into it and edit the information that changes and enter new information you may not have had at the start of writing the business plan.

❖ Jot down the major questions you need to answer about your business.

Notes :
_____
_____
_____
_____
_____
_____
_____

STEP 6.

Step 6. Register Your Business

Register your business with your state AND, if necessary, your county (parish if in Louisiana). Understand your state and county business requirements for business registration.

This is the first thing you need to do to legitimize your business.

Otherwise, how can you say you own a business when legally it does not exist?

Why you should register your business.

- It gives your business a unique identity while protecting it at the same time.
- Arguably one of the main reasons, registering your business protects you from personal liability.
- It attracts more customers, especially from the corporate world, because it is legit.
- Getting bank credits and capital from investors becomes easier.
- For generational continuity.

Gold Tip: Find out if your state makes you register in your county as well. For example, my skincare business is registered through my state, but I also am required to pay county taxes, so I had to register the business with my county, however, my county can also obtain my business registration information from the state if necessary.

❖ Visit your state business registration website and note any requirements they have that are necessary for you to register your business.

Notes :

_____

_____

_____

_____

_____

_____

STEP 7.

Step 7. Obtain your EIN or ITIN

Legitimize your business by getting your tax identification number.

Businesses with tax IDs enjoy more advantages compared to those without tax IDs. The Internal Revenue Service is the body responsible for issuing the 9-digit tax ID number, also known as the Employer Identification Number (EIN).

What's the difference between EIN and ITIN?

People who do not qualify for a Social Security Number (SSN) are required to have the Individual Taxpayer Identification Number (ITIN) for processing of taxes, while Employer Identification Number (EIN) is the tax processing number for the majority of businesses.

They all are tax identification numbers; the only difference is that they are used by different entities.

If you are a business owner and are not eligible for an SSN, then the alternative is the ITIN. With it, you can still file for your tax returns.

Types of Identification numbers

The Tax Identification Number is a collective term that may refer to any of the following:

- Employer Identification Number.
- SSN.
- ITIN.

- Adoption Tax Identification Number.

Where do you get one?

The simplest way to get a Tax ID is to apply through the IRS website.

The IRS's Interactive Tax Assistant tool is available for you if you need help figuring out whether or not you need to apply for the ITIN.

Why is this important?

You are a business earning revenue, so you will have to file taxes eventually. If you want to get a business account at a financial institution, you will need a tax ID number. You may also need a tax ID number for loans.

Without a tax ID, the types of business you can engage in will be limited. You cannot operate a corporation or a partnership without a tax identification number.

A business with a tax identification number has advantages. The owners are protected from debt and even certain liability. If it is a partnership, the owners enjoy the pass-through taxation.

When you decide to hire, you will need to have an EIN. You will need an EIN to report taxes and other documents to the IRS for yourself and your workers.

❖ A tax identification number is necessary for your business. Visit the IRS website and write down any additional requirements you may need to obtain your tax identification number.

Notes :
_____
_____
_____
_____
_____
_____
_____

STEP 8.

Step 8. Trademarks, Copyright, Patents, Licenses, Certifications, etc.

Gain Ownership of your Brand or Specific Products

A smart business owner must ensure that their brand is proprietary. If you do not, your competitors will be quick to rip off the results of your investment.

Trademarking

What do you trademark?

You can trademark your business or product name, the logo you designed, or even the labels of your products. When your brand has been trademarked, you gain exclusive rights to use it in connection with the registered services and goods.

When you have trademarked your brand, the Federal Courts allow you to file a lawsuit to protect it. However, you are the one responsible for monitoring and stopping any unauthorized use of whatever you have trademarked.

Why is trademarking important?

- People will be less likely to use a brand name/item that has already been trademarked.
- You will have the power to file for a lawsuit to enforce it.
- You will have the power to sue someone who trademarks or claims something you already own.
- You may be allowed to register anything you trademark outside the country as well.
- Trademarking gives you the right to use the ™ symbol of trademark. This tells people there is a trademark in progress or that you intend on trademarking. Once your trademark is officially registered, you have the right to use the ® symbol.
- Once you trademark something, the information is stored in the United States Patent and Trademark Office (USPTO) database so that a public record exists, showing ownership of the brand.

Copyrighting

When and what do you copyright?

Copyright protection applies to creative work. Contrary to popular belief, you can only copyright written works such as music, lyrics, blogs, scripts, books, photography, etc.

First, you must prove three things:

- The work is 100% original.
- You created it.
- The work is written in a tangible medium.

Why is copywriting important?

- Copyrights promote learning and creativity.
- It protects the work of authors by giving them exclusive rights to their work.
- It gives an author's work longevity; that is, ownership rights apply even after they die.
- They protect your work in the US and the world at large.
- They give authors the right to file penalties for copyright infringement.

Patents

When and what do you patent?

Patents apply to things that have been invented. Patents are costly and time-consuming. Still, if you have invented something, you must patent it immediately.

Why is it important to patent?

- Patents give you protection against copying/stealing by other competitors.
- If a person patents your invention before you, you will lose ownership rights to it.
- Because you are the exclusive owner of your invention, you will have a better market position because your competitors cannot claim what you own.
- Even without the resources, with a patent, many people are usually willing to help you turn your ideas into reality.
- A patent portfolio proves that you have technical expertise, something many investors appreciate.

Permits, Licenses, and Certifications

Depending on the type of business you carry out, your state or county may require specific licenses or certification for you to do business. You must understand which permits, licenses, or certifications your state requires for your business type, if applicable.

For example, you may need a permit to serve alcohol if you have a bar or restaurant with alcoholic beverages on the menu. Your bartenders or servers may need to be licensed to serve alcoholic beverages. These are things you must have BEFORE you are officially in business.

❖ Think about your business. Are there any specific certifications or licenses that you may need to do your business? Do a quick search to see if specific certifications or licenses are required for your business in your state or county.

Notes :

_____
_____
_____
_____
_____
_____
_____

STEP 9.

Step 9. Lawyer Up and Protect your Business

You need legal help. You need business insurance.

You will need an attorney and business insurance. I am just going to put that out there. You must protect your business as much as possible.

> **Business Insurance** - You will need business insurance. Depending on the type of industry, your insurance coverage requirements may vary. Be sure to shop around for affordable rates and coverage that will benefit your business.

❖ Call and shop around for different business insurance quotes. You will need to explain to the insurance broker what your business engages in to determine if they can quote and/ or cover your business. Below, write down different insurance agencies and the quotes they have provided you. Then, compare them to figure out the one that best fits your business needs.

Note that if you have a brick-and-mortar business and you are renting the space from a landlord, they may have certain business insurance requirements concerning the lease agreement you sign with them.

Notes :

_____
_____
_____
_____
_____
_____
_____

Why having an attorney is important for your business?

Don't wait until it's too late and you're being sued. Do not put off hiring a lawyer until you are being summoned by the courts. A  good business lawyer can protect you from mistakes before they even happen, saving you time and money, both valuable resources to your business.

You cannot afford to wait until you are paying settlements, attorney fees, and court fines before taking control of your business's legal affairs.

The American legal system is twisted. Getting sued is easy, but once you have been "trapped" there, it is extremely hard to get out. People hate attorney fees. However, the fee a lawyer will charge you to keep you out of trouble is very small compared to what the attorney will charge to get you out of trouble.

Things you may consider hiring an attorney for:

- Business registration and entity set up.
- Trademarking, patents, copyrights, etc.
- Basic zoning compliance.
- Website terms and conditions and privacy policies (if applicable to what you are doing).
- Legal agreement drafting. I highly recommend this if you consider having a partner or collaborator that influences your service or product to a broad audience.

❖ You should protect your business. Research some business attorneys in your area. Check to see if they do free consultations and explain what services you need from them. Write down the different attorneys in the note section below, their fees, and compare them to determine which one best fits your business needs.

Notes :

_____

_____

_____

_____

_____

_____

STEP 10.

Step 10. Don't Mix Business with Pleasure

Get a Business Bank Account.

Find a business account with no or low monthly fees. You're a new business, so try to save anywhere you can. Watch out for accounts with penalties for not meeting specific monthly account requirements.

Don't mix business revenue with personal revenue.

Not only is it unprofessional, but mixing business revenue with personal revenue is a prime target for scrutiny in IRS audits. This is a big mistake most entrepreneurs make.

If you want the IRS to take your business seriously, you must separate these two revenues. When they perceive your business as more of a *hobby* because your finances are not in place, they may quickly deny you any deductions and losses.

Without the clear separation of business deduction and personal revenue, you will not be able to claim expenses as deductions. How will you prove that the deductions you made were for business purposes alone? It will be easier to claim these deductions if your expenses are separated.

❖ Use this section to jot down expenses and reasons that you will need a business account. For example, you need a business account for incoming money from sales, to pay business expenses, etc.

Notes :

_____
_____
_____
_____
_____
_____
_____

STEP 11.

Step 11. Set up Reliable Payment Systems

Your small business is dependent on the client's ability to pay regularly and on time. This can only happen if you make and receive payments securely.

You can set up payment options in the following ways:

- Debit and credit cards.
- Automated Clearing House (ACH) processing.
- Recurring billing subscriptions.
- Stripe, PayPal, and Square.
- Contactless payments.

People must be able to securely pay you.

Some pre-built websites have secure payment gateways already set up, such as Shopify, Wix, etc., and all you must do is set up your preferred gateway account information for payments from orders to be sent directly into your account.

If you have a custom website built, you will need to sign up for a different payment system, like Stripe, and link your bank account information to that payment system. Your website developer will take the Application Programming Interface (API) code from the payment system you have set up and code it into your website.

❖ Think about the easiest way to receive payments from your customers and write them down in the note section below. For example, consider Stripe, PayPal, etc. when getting your website together.

Notes :
_____
_____
_____
_____
_____
_____
_____

STEP 12.

Step 12. Online Presence

Create an online presence.

An online presence reinforces your brand and markets the services and products you are offering in the market. You can be sure that quality online marketing will drive in many customers who may never have heard of your product.

An online presence also gives your brand credibility.

Create a website.

Use pre-built template websites or have a custom-designed website.

Design your social media accounts, or outsource this task to a professional.

❖ Think about the kind of website you need and write it down in the note section below. Is it a blog website, e-commerce website, etc.? Consider if you are trying to have clients book appointments or if you need to sell products.

Notes :
_____
_____
_____
_____
_____
_____
_____

Conclusion

In this book, you have learned how to:

- Step 1: Determine if you have a service business or a product business.
- Step 2: Create your business name.
- Step 3: Obtain your business domain.
- Step 4: Create your social media platforms.
- Step 5: Write your business plan.
- Step 6: Register your business.
- Step 7: Obtain your EIN or ITIN.
- Step 8: Obtain ownership of your specific brand or product (if necessary).
- Step 9: Seek out legal counsel (if necessary).
- Step 10: Obtain a business account.
- Step 11: Ensure customers can make secure payments.
- Step 12: Create your online presence, such as your website.

Gold Tip: The goal of this book was to guide you step-by-step to form your business. Please note that the steps sometimes must be done out of order, depending on the situation. For example, if you are unable to register a business yourself, you may first do Step 9 (Seeking out legal counsel) to assist you with Step 6 (Register your business), and that is perfectly okay.

Get a business mentor if you can. A business mentor can be someone proficient in many areas of business formation.

Thank you for reading The Left Behind Millennial: Business Formation Simplified. The point of this book is to guide you in the right direction to having a successful business.

You now have the tools to go start your own successful business.

Best of luck to you!

Siji Olufunwa

The remaining pages are here for any additional notes you may need to take.

Notes :

_____

_____

_____

_____

_____

_____

_____

_____

_____

_____

_____

_____

_____

_____

_____

_____

_____

_____

_____

_____

_____

_____

_____

_____

_____

_____

Notes :

**We'd love your feedback.

Like many of our readers, you may have found our readers' reviews important in making your decision to read this book. We would love it if you added your voice to the mix.

Please leave us a review and share your feedback on our book details page.

JOIN US ON SOCIAL MEDIA

@TLBMILLENNIAL

LIKE   **FOLLOW**   **SHARE**

References

Links

1. https://accounts.google.com/signup/v2/webcreateaccount?hl=en&flow Name=GlifWebSignIn&flowEntry=SignUp
2. https://domains.google/
3. https://play.google.com/store/apps/details?id=com.snapchat.android& hl=en&gl=US
4. https://us.godaddy.com/
5. https://web.facebook.com/?_rdc=1&_rdr
6. https://www.instagram.com/
7. https://www.linkedin.com/company/linkedin/
8. https://www.liveplan.com
9. https://www.namecheap.com/
10. https://www.pinterest.com/
11. https://www.tiktok.com/
12. https://twitter.com/home
13. https://www.youtube.com/

Websites

1. Brenner, M., (2018, August 9). Why Social Media Is Important for Business Marketing Retrieved from https://marketinginsidergroup.com/content-marketing/why-social-media-is-important-for-business-marketing/

2. Entrepreneur Press, E.P. *Starting a Business: The Idea Phase*. Retrieved from https://www.entrepreneur.com/article/217368

3. Evolve Creative, E.V. Why your brand name is important and reflects who you are.
   Retrieved from https://www.evolvecreative.com/why-your-brand-name-is-important-and-reflects-who-you-

are/#:~:text=It's%20vital%20that%20the%20name,relevant%20as%20y
our%20company%20evolves

4. ITIN W7 document preparation. *What is the difference between ITIN and EIN*? Retrieved from
   https://www.itin-w7-application.com/faqs/what-is-the-difference-
   between-itin-and-
   ein#:~:text=An%20Individual%20Taxpayer%20Identification%20Numbe
   r,tax%20processing%20number%20for%20businesses

5. Kjerulf, A. (2014, May 26). 5 Ways Hating Your Job Can Ruin Your Health (According to Science). Retrieved from
   https://www.huffpost.com/entry/happiness-tips_b_5001073

6. Lex Artifex, LLP. Importance of business registration: 9 reasons why you should register your business. Retrieved from
   http://www.lexartifexllp.com/importance-of-business-registration/

7. Peak, S., (2019, September 19). Understanding the Difference Between Product Businesses vs. Service Businesses. Retrieved from
   https://www.uschamber.com/co/grow/sales/differences-in-selling-
   products-and-services

8. Stahl, A. Hate your job? Here's what it's costing you. Retrieved from
   https://www.forbes.com/sites/ashleystahl/2016/03/03/hate-your-job-
   heres-what-its-costing-you/?sh=7dcfbfff6630

9. Wave Blog, (2019, May 1st). *The importance of a business plan*. Retrieved
   https://www.waveapps.com/blog/entrepreneurship/importance-of-a-
   business-plan

10. Wp beginner, (2020. November 16). Beginner's Guide: What is a Domain Name and How Do Domains Work? Retrieved from

https://www.wpbeginner.com/beginners-guide/beginners-guide-what-is-a-domain-name-and-how-do-domains-work/